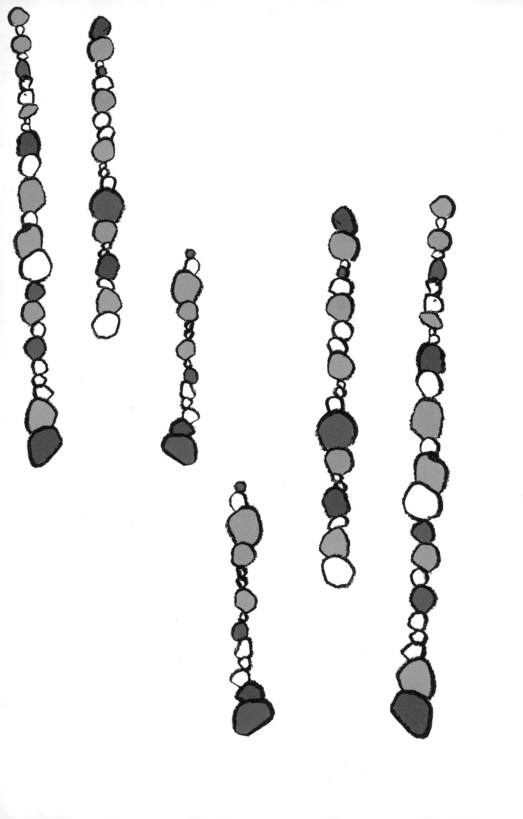

BE/HOLD
a friendship book

Shira Erlichman

penny
candy
BOOKS

Penny Candy Books
Oklahoma City & Savannah

Text & illustrations © 2019 Shira Erlichman

Photo of Shira: Hieu Minh Nguyen
Design: Shanna Compton

23 22 21 20 19   1 2 3 4 5
ISBN-13: 978-0-9996584-2-0 (hardcover)

Small press. Big conversations.
www.pennycandybooks.com

This book is dedicated to Angel, my of course.

Sweetheart, sometimes
when I'm feeling blue
I put my ear to the wind
and listen for you.

And suddenly I hear a boombox exploding with your voice.

Some might call it a windbox . . . or a songbox . . . or a wowbox . . .

and they'd be right. Some people can't hear a voice on the wind.

But I can.

I hear you sing a honeysong,
your voice full of bumblebees
zigging and zagging
every-which-way.

Your voice is a nightjar, spilling.

If somebody says,
"You can't hear a friend in a bumblebee!"
teach that poor nobody how to be a yesbody.
Tell them, listen, listen . . .

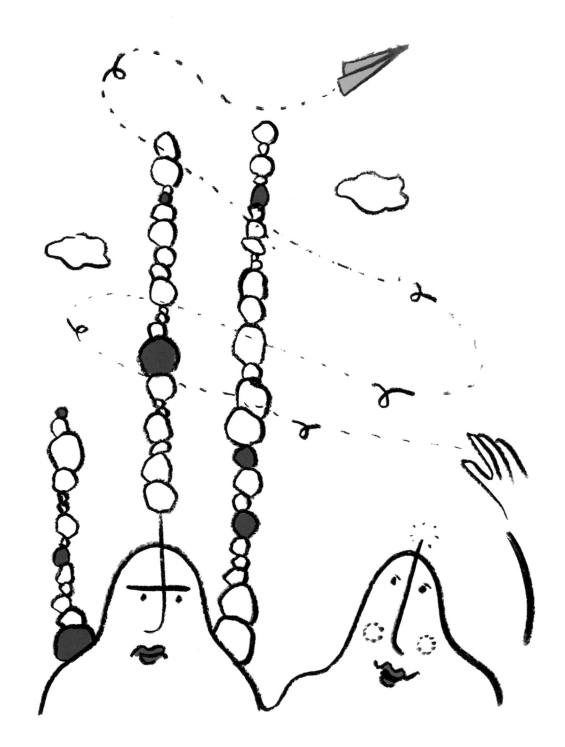

Be

Hold

Make

Believe

Life is a seesaw.
Sometimes you're up high,
sometimes you're down low.

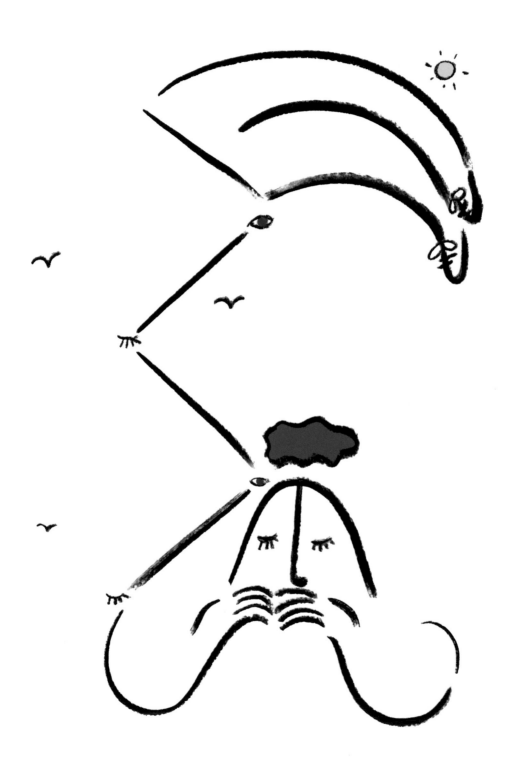

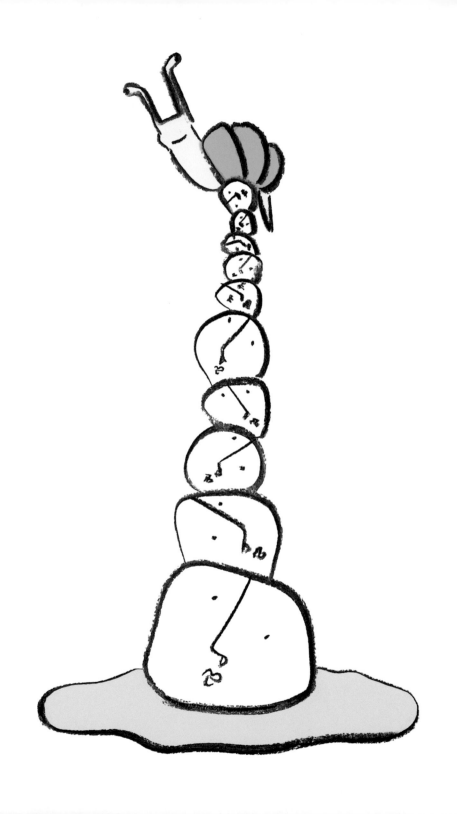

So why not invite someone
into your neighborhood?

That someone could be a slowpoke,
a daddy longlegs, or a sunset.

Even a downpour, a nightmare, or
an ice cream's melt.

They all deserve to be held.

Not with your hands, sweetpea,
but from deep within.

Take a breath.
Shrug your shape.
Let your heartstrings play.

Unleash a jar of jellybeans.
Put on your moonscreen.
Hula-hoop!
Slip a starfish in your pocket.

It's not easy to be brave.
The waves are high, the sea is dark.
But come, become with me.

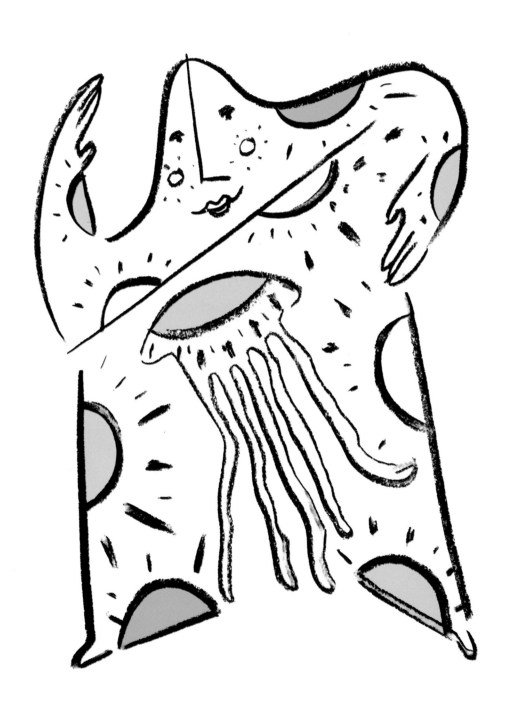

You have a light in you
like a lighthouse or a jellyfish.

and if you get overwhelmed and overflow,
I'll be your touchstone.
I'll be a whole riverbed of touches.

My hands can be your hands.
If you asked, I'd even brush your teeth.

You can count on me
to help you be

and hold.

I love where we overlap.

Life's no cakewalk. It's got its flaws.

But I'll bring the milkshake
if you bring two straws.

A friendship is like that.
With sails powered by
the deepest of breaths.

Some might call it a loveship . . .
or a songship . . . or a wowship . . .
and they'd be right.

But even if your ship's makeshift,
come beloved, be loved
by me.

There are earths to quake and sees to saw.
There's sand to quick and bones to wish.
Don't be tooscared. Be toocared.

Be so full of care, you're carefree.

You and me? We have superpowers.
We are the best togetherword.
Like bookworm, honeycomb, or sunflower.

Sometimes you might feel your brainstorm thundering.

Sometimes you might feel your brainclouds clear.

Sometimes it will go so dark
you'll wonder where your power went.

Some afternoons the mailman
won't bring a single letter.
It will feel like there's nothing to hold.

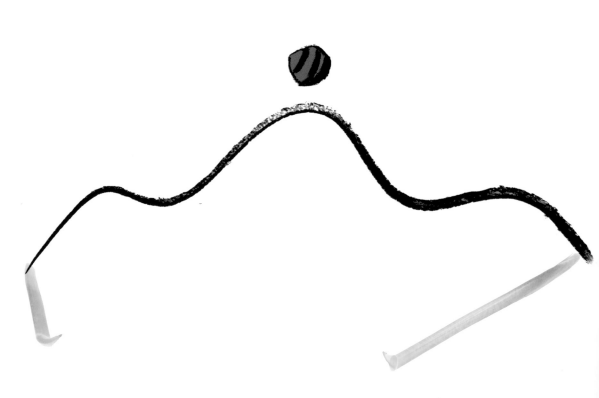

When this happens, find the simple, and keep it close.

Even the smallest stone
knows what a mountain knows.

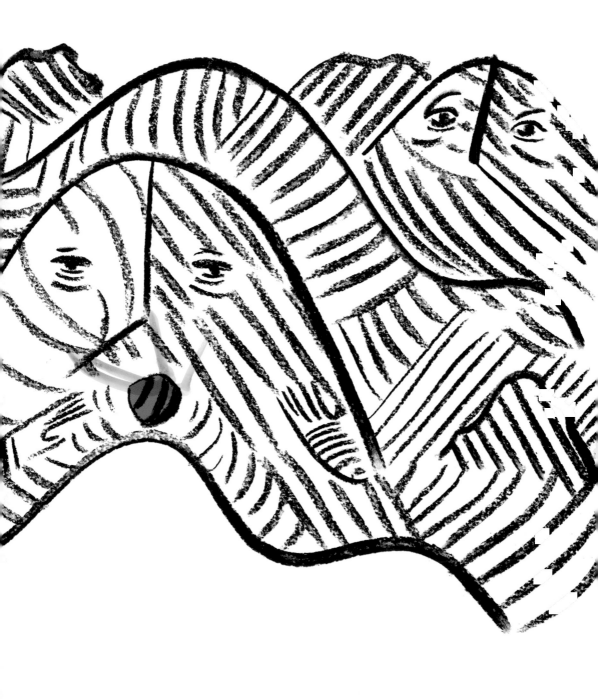

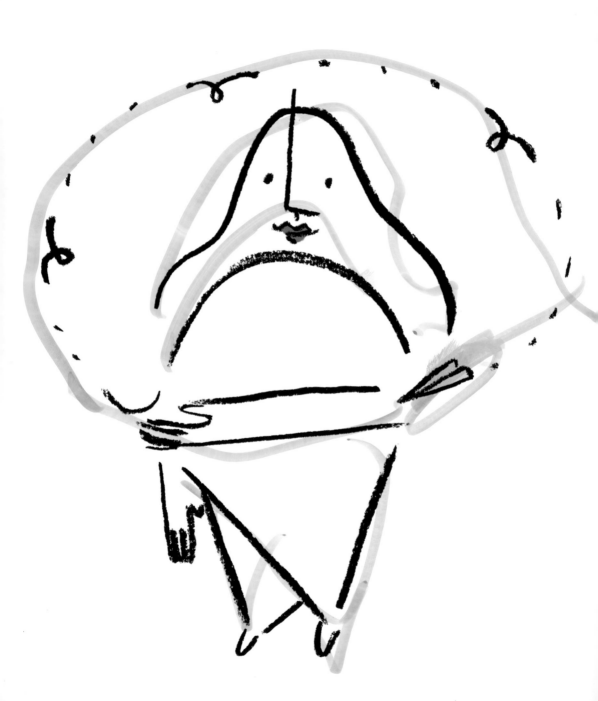

Even the tiniest yes
can lead to a WOOHOO!
If a yes likes you enough,
it sticks around.

One seed can grow
a forest of yesses.

And remember, you'll always belong.

AFTERWORD

This is a book about friendship. You may have noticed all of the compound words! That was very purposeful. A compound word takes two different words and puts them together to make a brand new word. In other words, it creates a friendship. It teaches us how to come together. A good friend invites another to be fully themselves, to share space and feelings, to contribute their own unique qualities. Friendship, like compound words, illuminates how much more interesting and vibrant life is when we unite.

A compound word is the smallest poem in the English language. Riverbed, awestruck, hammerhead, eyelash, hopscotch, highrise, sandcastle—once you start to notice them, they're everywhere! When I first really grasped *seesaw*, I was amazed. When you're at the top you *see*, when you're back at the bottom, you *saw*. It could've been called anything, but someone had the imagination to squish two verbs together. This is what poems do: compress experience. They take something as ordinary as a playground structure and reveal what's true and special about it. What if you're blind and ride the seesaw? You could call it a *feelfelt* or a *gowent* or an *updown*. You get to invent its name. Call it what feels true to you.

I am a compound word. As a six-year-old I immigrated from Israel to the United States of America. Suddenly, I was Israeli-American. What was that? I had a new home, but also a home that was far away. I walked into the words that were given to me. But words are never just words. They are homemakers and homebreakers.

Home is a small word, but it is a huge idea; it can be as simple as a person who cares for you or as complex as the land you grow up on. I love the compound *homebody* because it makes me think of my home as my body, my body as my home. What a good place to start. The bodies in this book are homebodies, yesbodies, nobodies, allbodies. They want a world where we all belong, where we challenge the words given to us.

I like to make up my own compound words. In first grade, we had to keep a moon journal. I learned that the moon could be "full" but not empty. It could be "new" but not old. In moon language the moon had "phases," not to be confused with faces. I saw that words were tricksters and began paying even closer attention to them. So I make up compound words all the time. It's fun to imagine new possibilities to describe the world around (and within) me.

Compounds are little odes. They honor the creativity it takes to merge many truths. Sometimes, because I was an immigrant, I was treated differently. But when people failed me, language didn't. When rules of identity failed me, imagination didn't. Language can be an affirmation of the complexities of life, a celebration of contradiction.

Compounds are rule-breakers. They're defiant and inventive. Up and lift becomes uplift. Sweet and heart becomes sweetheart. Language is magic—and it's yours, magician! When I first really considered the compound *behold*, I was stopped in my tracks. To behold is to simultaneously be *and* hold. It is stillness *and* activity. It is presence and permission. Let go and carry. Life can be challenging. Learning to be/hold can keep us grounded and open.

Even as I've become a grown up (hmm, am I a "grown up" or a "grown through?") I continue to take my favorite children's books off the shelf for consultation and comfort. Children's books are for *everyone*. Their gentleness, humanity, and playfulness can serve as reminders for traversing life's upsets and downpours. The voice of a successful children's book speaks to the very best part inside of us. It waters us. It addresses our knowing *and* our potential.

Here's to the very best part inside of you, which is both sun and flower, both be and long. I hope you find a friend (or two! or three!) in this book. And always remember how powerful you are.

With maple syrup,
Shira

In Hebrew *shira* means poem and song. True to her name, **Shira Erlichman** loves to write poems and sing songs. She also loves to draw pictures. Shira's art can be found in the *Huffington Post*, *PBS NewsHour's Poetry Series*, the *Rumpus*, on sidewalks, in living rooms, and in your boombox. She immigrated from Israel to the US when she was six and now lives in Brooklyn where she teaches and creates. Her favorite compound word is *seesaw*. Learn more at www.officialshira.com.

Create your own new compound words

FLIP	FLOP
TOOTH	BRUSH
GRAND	MA
HAMMER	HEAD
DOOR	BELL
SOUND	PROOF
HORSE	POWER
PAPER	PLANE
NIGHT	MARE
HOME	BODY
SWEET	HEART
QUICK	SAND
HONEY	MOON

My new compound words

HONEYHEAD

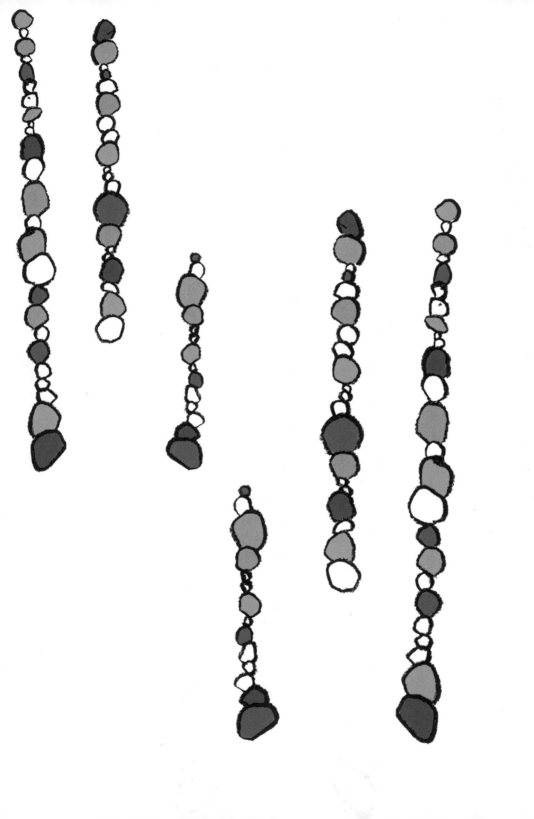